New Vanguard • 133

British Mark IV Tank

David Fletcher • Illustrated by Tony Bryan

First published in Great Britain in 2007 by Osprey Publishing,
Midland House, West Way, Botley, Oxford OX2 0PH, UK
443 Park Avenue South, New York, NY 10016, USA
E-mail: info@ospreypublishing.com

A CIP catalogue record for this book is available from the British Library

ISBN: 978 1 84603 082 6

Page layout by Melissa Orrom Swan, Oxford
Index by Alan Thatcher
Typeset in Helvetica Neue and ITC New Baskerville
Originated by PPS Grasmere Ltd, Leeds, UK
Printed in China through Worldprint Ltd.

07 08 09 10 11   10 9 8 7 6 5 4 3 2 1

For a catalogue of all books published by Osprey Military and Aviation
please contact:

NORTH AMERICA
Osprey Direct, c/o Random House Distribution Center, 400 Hahn Road,
Westminster, MD 21157
E-mail: info@ospreydirect.com

ALL OTHER REGIONS
Osprey Direct UK, P.O. Box 140 Wellingborough, Northants, NN8 2FA, UK
E-mail: info@ospreydirect.co.uk

www.ospreypublishing.com

Editor's note

Unless otherwise stated, all images are courtesy of the Tank Museum,
Bovington, UK

BRITISH MARK IV TANK

THE FIRST MAIN BATTLE TANK

The Mark IV could probably be described as the first Main Battle Tank. Some 1,200 were built and they participated in virtually every British battle on the Western Front from the early summer of 1917 until the very end of the war, plus one action in the Middle East. Apart from its mass production, the Mark IV was also the first tank to be built based upon experience with earlier tanks and the first to be used en masse in combat, in a battle actually planned around the tank. Even so, it could have been a far better machine had it not been for a serious clash of personalities.

The Mark IV was based, mechanically, on the prototype tank *Mother*, which in an ideal world should have been improved upon by 1917. The problem was the eternal conflict between the ideal and the expedient. Everyone agreed that the four-man driving system, introduced with *Mother* in 1915, was tiresome and inefficient, but what to do about it? Lt Walter Wilson knew the answer, but Maj Albert Stern, head of the Mechanical Warfare Department, overruled him. Lacking technical acumen, and unable to see the brilliant simplicity of Wilson's scheme, Stern ordered this first production tank to use the same system as *Mother*, while experiments were carried out to find the most effective form of transmission. The matter was decided in favour of Wilson's design in competitive trials at Oldbury in March 1917, but that was too late to influence the Mark IV. Stern had unwittingly managed to delay the improvement of British tanks by a good 18 months.

King George V and BrigGen Hugh Elles watch two new Mark IV tanks on a steeplechase course at Neuve Eglise in July 1917, the month that the Tank Corps came into being. The event provides a fine comparison between male and female models.

Haig's order

Readers of our title on the Mark I tank (Osprey New Vanguard 100) will recall that, immediately after the very first tank attack in September 1916, General Haig placed an order for 1,000 more. These would appear in due course as the Mark IV. Meanwhile the surviving Mark Is would have to soldier on. They were supplemented by small production runs of Mark II and Mark III machines, which would be required to train the new army of tank crews to be raised for the Mark IV. It is difficult, today, to appreciate the implications of Haig's order. British manufacturing industries were already groaning under the strain of war. The great shell scandal that could have brought the British Army to its knees in 1915 was only slowly being overcome, now that dozens more firms had taken up the work. The British railway system was nearly falling apart as it struggled to meet increased demand and the shipbuilding industry was working to full capacity, endeavouring to produce more warships and replace merchant vessels lost through enemy action. On top of these conditions there was an increasing demand for aircraft, transport vehicles, rifles, grenades, mortars and all the other materiel of war.

The numbers game

Production of Mark IV tanks got underway in March 1917 as soon as the last Mark II and Mark III machines were finished. Deliveries were soon running at about 20 tanks per week, although it was hoped that double this number would be produced. Not everything was running smoothly. Considerable confusion followed the placing of the 1,000-tank order and it was not settled until the Prime Minister intervened, at which point the War Office took a more optimistic view and authorized what amounted to an open-ended order. At one stage the total number of Mark IV tanks on order was 1,400. Ordering like this was a risky business. It should have been a foregone conclusion that improved designs would appear, indeed the Oldbury Trials had only recently guaranteed this. So orders assuming that the present type would be manufactured for an infinite future threatened to clog existing production facilities, probably at a critical time.

The initial confusion over quantities is reflected in a good deal of uncertainty over individual orders as to who got what and how many tanks each firm would actually build. Overall, out of the total of 1,400 the following is believed to be an accurate breakdown:

Cancelled	180
Fighting tanks	950
Supply tanks	205
Experimentals	11
Surplus	54

Therefore, of the 1,220 Mark IVs actually built 1,155 were available for combat or training, if one includes the supply tanks. As we shall see, far more Mark IV tanks were ultimately used for experimental purposes than those shown here, and were presumably earmarked for this role from the outset. Whether the others were adapted from redundant service tanks or the surplus stock is not clear. Other figures suggest that of the 1,015 fighting, experimental and surplus tanks – that is excluding supply tanks – 420 were completed as male machines and 595 as female.

Since it was fair to assume that any firm not engaged upon war work by 1916 was not much good, the only answer to increased production was to spread the work around amongst those that were good. The main contractor would still be the Metropolitan Carriage, Wagon & Finance Company of Birmingham, and Fosters of Lincoln would take its share, but other firms were brought in, notably Beardmores, the Coventry Ordnance Works and Mirrlees Watson in Glasgow, plus Armstrong-Whitworth in Newcastle-upon-Tyne. Sub-contractors would also be drawn in: the Daimler Motor Company, understandably, for engines, gearboxes and differentials, and others like the Glasgow firms Hurst, Nelson Ltd and John Brown & Company, which assembled tank hulls for parent contractors.

Haig's great hope was to have enough new tanks available for a proposed offensive in the spring of 1917, but for a variety of reasons there were delays that combined to frustrate this plan. Raw materials were in short supply, new contractors had to be educated and there were numerous design changes to be worked out and incorporated, although some had been foreshadowed in the Mark II and III.

A Mark IV female fitted with a portable tank crane lifts heavy items onto light railway wagons, probably at the depot in France. The jib is secured to the back of the cab and employs a manual chain hoist.

THE MARK IV DESCRIBED

Perhaps the simplest way to describe those things that changed and those that did not would be to compare the Mark IV with the Mark I, starting at the front.

The process of up-armouring successive types of tank started in a very modest way. The practice began with the Mark II and was standardized on the Mark IV. The front of the Mark IV's cab remained at 12mm, but the area covered by 8mm plate was extended along the sides in order to provide better protection for the crew and the main mechanical components. The less vulnerable areas beneath the tank and at the rear remained at 6mm thickness. Little could be done to improve the quality of armour. The science of producing thin, bullet-proof plate was still in its infancy; the plate still had to be worked by rather old-fashioned tools and a fair amount had to be rejected as inadequate or too brittle.

The layout of the cab front, one of the best guides to accurate identification of the different marks, was nearly identical to that of the Mark III. The cab was narrower than the original Mark I version in order to leave room for wider track plates, once these became available, but this feature had been introduced with the Mark II. Hinged visors for the driver and steersman remained the same and the vision slits directly above them were tucked up beneath the lip of the angle iron running along the top of the cab – here is the place to look for a difference. Insignificant as it may be, it is the spacing of the rivets along this strip that conclusively identifies a Mark IV from Marks II and III. On the latter vehicles a pair of rivets will be found at each end of the strip, closer together than the rest. On the Mark IV the rivets are all equally spaced. This pattern is repeated on the angle iron at the rear of the cab roof.

What this design difference reveals is important. It shows that new armour plate jigs had been prepared for the Mark IV, whereas the interim Marks II and III were built on and adapted from the old Mark I tank jigs. For example, the sloping plate below the cab front was now plain; there was no sign at all of the large bolts or filled bolt holes indicating where the tail steering wheel was located on the Mark I.

A close look at the front plate showing the two-stage hinged visors, the vision slots and the plugged ball mounting for the Lewis gun. The rivet and bolt arrangement along the top is a significant identification feature of the Mark IV. The brackets on top were intended to be supports for camouflage.

Another change relates to the machine-gun armament, which will be covered in more detail later. As ever, preliminary evidence is visible on the Mark III with the appearance of a large, round opening between the two visors, which was designed to accommodate a ball mounting for the Lewis gun instead of the narrow slot provided for the Hotchkiss.

No change is evident in the tracks. The wider type were not available until 1918 and, if photographic evidence is any guide, none were ever fitted to the Mark IV. However, based upon experience with the Mark I the front idlers, or track-adjusting wheels, were smooth rather than fitted with teeth to engage the tracks, a configuration that caused endless problems. Among various criticisms of the original design by the engineer and Tank Corps officer Philip Johnson was one concerning the robustness of the track rollers. As originally built these were hollow and, on occasions when a lot of weight was brought to bear upon a few of them, as when passing over a fallen tree for example, they could collapse. A temporary remedy involved filling them, but on the Mark IV and all subsequent tanks they were manufactured in a solid state.

Looking now at the top of the Mark IV, behind the cab, there are a number of significant differences to note. Most important of all was the provision of a silencer for the engine exhaust system. The lack of this simple device was a serious inconvenience for early tank crews. It was not just the noise that was the problem, although that was bad enough, but the great cloud of fumes from the Daimler engine that hung over each tank and at night a red glow and the occasional sparks from this area that gave the tank's position away. Everything had been tried from applications of wet mud to improvised silencers, but a type designed specifically for the engine was clearly the answer. It was aligned to cover the three exhaust outlets and ended in a long tail pipe that ran along the roof and down the back to end between the track horns. This system not only eliminated the noise and heat problem on top; it also dispersed the fumes in a less obvious place and, most important of all, reduced the external noise. Men present at the Cambrai battle in November 1917 often remarked on how quiet these tanks seemed to be when at rest or moving slowly with the engine on tick-over. It was quite a different matter inside, of course, but it

Front view of a Mark IV female at Beardmores in Glasgow. This view shows clearly the alternating flanged and unflanged rollers, the toothless idler wheels and the flanges, on the lower frames, which support the tracks.

did mean that tanks could crawl up to their start lines without too much risk of alerting the enemy.

The round hatch on top of the Mark I tank had already been replaced in the Mark II with what is often described as a trapezoid-shaped structure, and this was repeated on the Mark IV. If the tank's commander could be spared from his usual duty of operating the steering brakes he could, by standing on the gearbox cover behind the engine, raise the lid and have a look round in relative safety. At the rear, where the roof sloped down to meet the back plate, the manufacturers provided a stowage tray formed from side panels of light steel, and this was normally used to carry bulky items such as the camouflage net, towing cable, extra fuel cans and track extension plates when they were not fitted.

The wheeled steering tail had already been removed from surviving Mark I tanks and was never seen again on any service tanks. This arrangement released a space between the rear track horns, which was now given over to a vital improvement. Enclosed within an armoured box, low down at the rear, was a 318-litre (70-gallon) fuel tank that replaced the two 113-litre (25-gallon) tanks either side of the cab in earlier models. This tank was a considerable advance in terms of safety and it extended the potential distance the tank could run by an average 16km (10 miles). At the same time it gave the designers a new problem to solve. The original arrangement, dangerous as it was, enabled fuel to run by gravity feed to the carburettor. Now, with the fuel at a lower level, some form of delivery system was required. The original scheme seems to have been to employ an air pump, which was a standard fitting on the Daimler engine, but this was not entirely satisfactory, so a proprietary product known as the Autovac was installed which, as its name implies, worked on a vacuum principle.

Inside the tank there are other things to note. At the front, on either side of the cab where the fuel tanks had been, new features were installed – on the right an open storage space alongside the driver and on the left a locker for the officer and a container for drinking water. Even so, on active service, there was never enough room to stow everything that was required and the floor, on either side of the engine, would be cluttered with additional stores.

Photographed near Bapaume in September 1918, two Mark IV supply tanks move forward shrouded in clouds of exhaust fumes. The tank on the right tows a pair of supply sledges, while captured German infantry pick their way carefully in the opposite direction.

Weapons and sponsons

Changes of armament and the shape of the sponsons that mounted them are undoubtedly the most significant features of the Mark IV. In the male type there were two problems to be faced. One was supply; the original 'long' 6-pounder of the Mark I was still in demand for the Royal Navy and, indeed, it was a shortage of these weapons that led to the adoption of female tanks in the first place. Second, tank crews had discovered that the gun was too long. Not only was it easily clogged with mud if the tank leaned over too far on soft ground; it was also liable to damage from striking trees or man-made structures still standing on the battlefield that the crew, from inside, did not notice.

As a consequence a new weapon was designed, which was essentially a shortened version of the original. Known officially as the Ordnance Quick Firing 6-pounder 6 hundredweight Mark I, it had a barrel length, measured in calibres, of 23 instead of the 40 of the original weapon. This shortening amounts in practice to a substantial difference of 112.7cm (4½in.). Under normal circumstances this should result in a loss of accuracy at longer ranges and a lower muzzle velocity. In fact the former was not a problem since tanks engaged their targets at relatively close range and the effective muzzle velocity was little different. The reason for this was the fact that the longer guns, having been made as single tube, rather than by a built-up technique, to ease production, were limited to a lower charge for safety. The shorter gun was also single tube but a good deal thicker at the breech end so that the standard charge could be fired. Firing data for the 'short' gun included a maximum range of 6,675m (7,300 yards) at a muzzle velocity of 411.5m (1,350fps). Firing solid shot it was estimated that the gun could penetrate 30mm (1⅕in.) of armour at 457m (500 yards). High-explosive ammunition was also available.

A male sponson, starboard side. The short six-pounder gun in its rotating shield casts a shadow on the lower, more angular plates. Farther back is a Lewis gun in the ball mounting, looking massive. Notice that, in contrast to the Mark I, the door on a Mark IV male sponson swings outwards.

The new gun was adopted in January 1917, but it is likely that the design of the new male sponson may have anticipated this. Experience in the field had shown that the original male sponson, which was deep at both front and side, had a tendency to embed itself in mud when the tank was not running level. Of course, if there was one chore the crews cordially hated it was having to remove and re-attach these sponsons every time tanks had to be moved by rail, which was the normal method. Thus the new sponson was designed to be slightly smaller all round and more bevelled on the lower surfaces to avoid close contact with mud. This improvement, and the adoption of the shorter gun, meant that for rail journeys the sponsons could be closed up, inside the tank, in order to reduce the width.

Not that this procedure was a simple exercise. First, the guns had to be put on full elevation and the barrels run back as far as they would go. Then, in a sequence of prescribed moves, the two sponsons were unbolted and swung inboard one end at a time to be secured by a pin and clevis arrangement to the main engine bearers. There

The driver and brakeman were virtually trapped in the cab, which is why a roof hatch was later introduced, while the secondary gears could only be operated if the sponson doors were lifted off their hinges and stowed separately.

It is now generally accepted that the adoption of the Lewis light machine gun as the secondary weapon in male tanks and the main armament of females was a mistake. Undoubtedly the big, water-cooled Vickers used on the first tanks was too cumbersome and required a massive female sponson, but the Lewis gun, good as it was in the field, was not suited to tanks. The Lewis was an air-cooled gun that worked by drawing air through the barrel casing at the breech end, but this flow was reversed by the action of the tank's own cooling fan, which meant that warm air from the gun, along with fumes from the muzzle, flowed straight into the gunner's face every time it fired. It was not a disastrous failing but was by no means ideal, and the Tank Corps managed to live with it throughout 1917. The officer believed to be responsible for this change was LtCol Baker-Carr, a machine-gun expert who later commanded 1st Tank Brigade.

The Lewis gun was not only lighter than the Vickers, it hardly required a mounting, in the traditional sense, at all. What it did need was a fairly large aperture in the armour and this was resolved by designing a very effective form of ball mounting. Essentially this was a solid steel ball, with a hole big enough to accept the jacketed Lewis gun and a bit more for the sight. The ball moved freely within a phosphor bronze mounting so that the weapon could be aimed in any direction, and if the gun was withdrawn the ball would be turned sideways within the mounting, to seal it off entirely from the outside. One such mounting was provided in the cab front of both male and female tanks, another in each male sponson and two in each female sponson.

The design of the female sponson had already been seen on some Mark III tanks, but it was refined in the Mark IV. The upper part, with a gun mounting more or less at each end, was not unlike a small bow window in shape, but it was now in two halves so that it could be folded

This Mark IV, which rejoiced in the name of *Whiskey and Soda*, served in Ireland, where two young officers show it off to their lady friends. It may have been a rare example of a Mark IV hermaphrodite with a male sponson on the starboard side.

A new Mark IV male and some of its crew relaxing in the sun. Someone must be working on the engine; note one half of the engine cover leaning against the sponson. The 6-pounder gun tube has been run back as it would be when the sponson was withdrawn.

inwards from the centre sufficiently to clear the railway loading gauge. The lower part was filled in by a series of panels, two of which were hinged to open outwards. In theory, if the crew had to evacuate in a hurry they only had to kick release levers on the inside of these panels and roll out, clear of the tank. However, gruesome pictures from the aftermath of Cambrai show that sometimes even this was not enough.

Gunners on male tanks soon discovered that on the Western Front there was precious little above ground to shoot at. Since one had to stop the tank to ensure accuracy with the 6-pounder it was probably better to fire for effect and create a lot of noise than to actually try to hit anything. Most of the visible targets were human and machine guns were far more effective, since it did not matter very much whether the tank was moving or not when they were fired.

Building the tanks
Production of the Mark IV began in March 1917, some two months behind schedule. Despite the fact that the work was scattered in factories across England and Scotland, the big order involved a degree of standardization that might be seen as a form of mass production. The scheme involved building many parts of the tank as sub-assemblies before everything was brought together in the erecting shop for final assembly. This procedure involved the inner frames, with all connecting panels being assembled on jigs with the aid of power riveters before coming to the erecting shop, where hand riveting was employed to attach them to the floor and lower body panels. The outer frames were similarly assembled and then attached, and temporary long axles were used to line up the frames through the idler, secondary gear and sprocket holes. Meanwhile, the track rollers had been slotted into place so that their axles could be pushed through once the outer frames were fitted.

At this stage the tracks were laid out below the tank, which was then lowered onto them. Then the long axles were withdrawn while the gear wheels and sprockets were installed between the frames. The engine,

Hurst Nelson, a Glasgow-based rolling stock manufacturer, assembled Mark IV hulls for other Clydeside tank builders. The row of holes along the bottom will take track rollers and the large slots at the front show the location of the track tensioning fixtures.

gearbox, differential and control levers, which would have been delivered from the Daimler Company, were now lined up on a sub-frame and lowered into the tank from above, along with the radiator and fan assembly. Next the rear plate was riveted into place and the roof panels bolted on top; this so that they could be removed to enable an engine to be changed. Engineers now attached the final details, including various internal and external fittings, the petrol tank and, of course, the sponsons. Finally the tracks were joined up, a coat of paint was applied and the new tank was driven out of the erecting shop ready for delivery. At this stage the vehicle would be without any weapons, which were a War Office responsibility.

THE TANK CORPS EXPANDS

Clearly, as the number of tanks increased the way they were organized would have to change. It was no good simply expanding the number of companies without arranging some sort of structure to manage them. So in October 1916 it was announced that the four existing tank companies in France would be expanded and elevated to the status of battalions, while five new battalions would be raised at home. In November the title of the tank forces was changed from Heavy Section to Heavy Branch of the Machine Gun Corps, which presumably indicated greater independence, but it was all largely academic until the new tanks were ready.

In fact at this time, at least in Britain, the administration was more concerned with the transfer of the home training base from Thetford in Norfolk to Bovington Camp near the village of Wool in Dorset. Another administrative change in January 1917 saw the creation of the 1st Tank Brigade to oversee the activities of C and D battalions. This step was repeated in February when A and B battalions came under 2nd Tank Brigade.

C4 was a C Battalion tank, a female with a complicated pattern of dark lines painted on the sponson to conceal the vision slits. The crew, some in overalls, others in two-piece uniforms, are working on the tank which, bearing the name *Cyprus II,* fought at Cambrai.

The organization of a battalion went through numerous modifications on paper before it was confirmed. It would inevitably be a compromise between what was available in terms of tanks and men, and what was manageable in terms of structure and command. Finally, the authorities settled upon an arrangement whereby each battalion was split into three companies, but after that an element of choice appears to have crept in. For example, D Battalion's history is quite emphatic that throughout 1917 each company had three sections with four tanks per section (two male and two female if this could be arranged), whereas the history of G Battalion is equally clear that its companies were organized into four sections of three tanks each: one male and two female. Companies were numbered in continuing sequence so that A Battalion had 1st, 2nd and 3rd companies, B Battalion 4th, 5th and 6th and so on. Within the battalion, sections were numbered consecutively 1 through 9 or 12 and the tanks in the same way so that, for example, in A Battalion tank A1 would be the first of four tanks in the first of three sections in 1st Company. Not that it always worked out so neatly in practice. The first 76 Mark IV tanks to arrive in France were handed over to A and B battalions in 2nd Tank Brigade in May 1917 – they would be the first to take them into action.

Meanwhile, as they left the factories in Britain, new Mark IV tanks underwent a basic mechanical test on some adjacent site. In Birmingham, for example, this was at Oldbury, where men from 20 Squadron Royal Naval Air Service, maintaining the Admiralty link with 'Landships', put them through their paces in a large field that was soon churned into a landscape of mud. The new tanks were then taken by rail to Avonmouth, shipped around to Le Havre and then delivered, over the French railway system, to what became known as the Tankodrome at Erin, near St Pol, where they were tested again and prepared for service. Farther south, a section of the old trench system at Wailly, close to Arras, was acquired for use as a practical driving school. F (later 6th) Battalion was sent there on 1 June 1917, being newly arrived from Bovington. Here, according to its history, it took over a number of Mark IV tanks for driving instruction over the old German trenches. Tanks were not available for every crew so the work had to be done in shifts, but it was generally agreed that the training was invaluable.

INTO BATTLE

In Flanders field

The battle to take Messines Ridge was a curtain-raiser to Haig's plan for a summer offensive in Flanders, based around Ypres. The battle began on 7 June 1917 with a series of mines being set off beneath the German lines along a 16km (10-mile) stretch of the front. The results were so devastating that the infantry was able to swarm in at once, without much need for tanks which, in any case, were slowed down by the churned-up nature of the ground. Based on trials carried out against older tanks the Germans were ready for them with a new, armour-piercing bullet, known as the 'K' round, which was fired from the standard German service rifle. However, the improved armour protection of the Mark IV was sufficient to defeat this projectile and two tanks, which became ditched during the day's fighting, were struck repeatedly by these bullets but never penetrated.

Ditching was the term used to describe what happened when a tank became stuck. Even on good ground this could occur. A trench that was too wide, or approached in the wrong way, could easily trap a tank. So could a large shell hole, but if the ground was waterlogged, churned up by shell fire and turned into a bottomless swamp, it was likely that ditching would become the norm rather than the exception when a 28-ton tank was driven over it. Indeed, ditching became such a feature of the tank experience throughout that summer that it very nearly led to the total demise of the tank. Even if tanks could keep going through the slough they tended to sink so deep that it proved impossible to steer them, so they simply ploughed straight on until a shell hole or other obstacle stopped them. At this point most of the weight was being taken by the underbelly of the tank while the tracks flailed around impotently.

The first expedient for handling a ditched tank was to search the area around the stricken vehicle for anything that could be packed under the tracks to give a grip. Some tanks were provided with a device called the 'Torpedo Spud' that could be attached to a track at such times, but this

The scene alongside the rebuilt Menin Road shortly after the war showing the wrecks of three tanks that nearly made it across the swamp in the soggy summer of 1917. Over time they have been stripped of virtually every useful item.

was soon eclipsed by a far more effective device known as the unditching beam. It is believed to have been devised by Philip Johnson, then serving as an engineer officer at Erin. The beam itself was a solid piece of oak, protected by steel plates on two sides, which could be chained to the tracks and dragged around underneath the tank if it became ditched, in order to provide a firm purchase. Since the beam weighed in the region of 508kg (1,118lb) it was not easy to manhandle, so each tank was provided with a set of rails running from front to back along the top of the tank and high enough to clear the cab and other fittings. When not required the beam was carried on top of the tank and secured to these rails. Once the tank was stuck two crew members, each with pockets full of spanners, would climb onto the tank and attach the beam to the tracks by means of a sort of chain-and-stirrup arrangement. The driver would then put the tank in gear, lock the differential and use the beam to get out of the hole. On very bad ground some drivers kept going with the beam attached until they were safely onto firmer ground. Then the tank stopped, with the beam back on its rails, to be stowed for the next time. Bearing in mind that this was often done under fire, and sometimes more than once in a single action, the role of the volunteers who attached it is not to be envied. As a corollary to this it should be noted that once the unditching gear design was worked out a requirement was issued for the equipment to be manufactured in Britain. Since nobody would take on the job, pleading pressure of other work, Central Workshops in France made all the unditching gear for the Mark IV tanks, so it is reasonably safe to say that any Mark IV tank seen with the rails fitted had experienced service in France at one time or another.

On 27 July 1917 the Heavy Branch became the Tank Corps and thus severed its tenuous connection with the Machine Gun Corps. A new cap badge was adopted, bearing the motto *Fear Naught*, and as time went by other details were introduced to make the Tank Corps more distinctive in its own right. All of this took place literally to the sound of the guns, for on 16 July 1917 a huge bombardment began from a total of 3,091 guns

A famous picture taken in Peronne selected to show the stowed unditching beam, the vast number of spare petrol cans carried on the roof and the end of a towing cable at the back. It is also worth remarking how often tanks are seen with no obvious markings on display at all.

firing along an 18km (11-mile) front. Various matters conspired to cause this barrage to continue for the next 15 days, after which the battle known as Third Ypres began, as did the rain.

The Tank Corps had allocated 216 fighting tanks to the battle, shared between the six battalions then in France. Each battalion also had six supply tanks, issued on a scale of two per company, which at this time had been modified from redundant Mark I and Mark II machines. Third Ypres would have been a tragic battle whether tanks had been involved or not, but it would be wrong to suggest, as some accounts do, that they contributed nothing. The tanks shared the misery, learned a great deal and just now and then produced an impressive performance. Even so, in the main, it was a test of stamina for officers and men to launch their tanks upon a sea of mud and struggle forwards in the most appalling conditions in an effort to assist the infantry, who suffered far more.

It is from this period that another useful aid, known as the ashplant, can be dated. In place of the usual officer's cane Tank Corps officers took to carrying a longer stick, approximately 12.7mm (½in.) in diameter, which they used to test the ground. The simple test was that if it required two hands to push the stick 30–45cm (12–18in.) into the ground that equated to a bearing pressure of 1.4kg/sq cm (20psi), if just one hand was required to achieve the same effect that would represent 0.7kg/sq cm (10psi), but if the stick went right in up to the handle the ground could bear no more than 0.35kg/sq cm (5psi). Even sunk to its belly plates a Mark IV tank exerted a pressure of 5.skg (11.6psi). Of course, the deeper a tank sank into the ground the length of track in contact increased; typically, standing on

The 3rd Battalion tank *Crusty* provides us with a good view of the top. The bar above the cab seems to have broken loose from somewhere, but it is possible to see the number 24 (painted on top of the cab), the covers for the periscope holes, the silencer and roof hatch, which is open. Notice also the rear stowage position of the unditching beam and the mud that accumulates on top of the sponsons.

firm ground, the length of track in contact was 1.4m (4ft 7in.), but in motion on softer ground this would increase to 3.35m (11ft). There is some evidence to suggest that the experience of operating tanks in this mud introduced a change in the driving technique. Afterwards it seems the normal practice was to drive with the differential locked.

The first day of Third Ypres resulted in the ditching of more than 70 tanks and the loss of a substantial number to enemy artillery where ground conditions obliged the vehicles to follow one another along a particular route. It also led to the near suicidal practice by some officers of walking ahead of their tanks under fire, prodding the ground with their ashplants in order to keep them on a safe course. Yet in all of this there were highlights. On 19 August 1917, nine tanks took part in what appeared to be a desperate mission to capture the village of St Julien. Not that there was much to capture: St Julien was little more than a map reference where, in places, the mud was stained with the colour of bricks from demolished houses. Now the only buildings were reinforced concrete strongpoints which were the Flanders equivalent to the trenches of the Somme, since to dig trenches here was pointless unless one was looking for water.

Moving in line ahead and sticking to what remained of the roads, the tanks crossed a stream and drove into the village. Two bogged in the stream, but the remainder all attacked their objectives and by bold handling literally outgunned the strongpoints one after another. At the end five tanks were able to turn around and drive back to the British lines. The attack was launched without any preliminary bombardment but was shielded by a smoke screen, and the village was captured at a total cost of 15 casualties.

That success notwithstanding, the offensive dragged on until the beginning of November. Tanks were used on numerous occasions, but it was a costly offensive that never achieved its ultimate objective and nearly did for the tanks. As early as 3 August the Tank Corps' tactical expert, Maj J. F. C. Fuller, declared that the tank's part in the Ypres offensive was over. He argued for a new attack on ground more suitable to tanks, but others drew a different conclusion. Many officers, some of high rank, deduced that if tanks could not operate in the prevailing conditions then they were useless.

Operation *Hush*

Third Ypres was not just some pointless offensive, launched into the blue – it had important objectives. One was to drive German forces from the Flanders coast and capture the U-boat bases that were causing so much trouble to Allied shipping. In typically British tradition a scheme was hatched to launch an amphibious operation as a supplement to the main offensive. This was daring enough under the circumstances, but made more so by a decision to include some tanks in the attacking force, less than a year since they had first been used in action.

A special force was raised that included infantry, artillery and nine tanks. Secret training areas were prepared and special craft built. The scheme involved employing six shallow-draught, big-gun warships known as Monitors which, lashed together in pairs, would propel three long pontoons, each 167.6m (550ft) from stem to stern, up to the beach. Three tanks would be stationed at the head of each pontoon and they would lead

the forces ashore. The problem was that this low-lying coast was protected by a high sea wall, shaped in places like a curling wave before it breaks, complete with a protruding crest.

After a great deal of experimental work a scheme was approved to overcome this obstacle. The first tanks ashore would each propel a wedge-shaped ramp up the wall until it lodged under the lip of the crest. The tank would then detach the ramp and clamber over it, using its guns to keep heads down once it reached the top. Since the wall was likely to be slippery with seaweed and slime, special spikes were fitted to the tracks so that the tanks could grip, but even this was not the end of the innovation. The sea wall would also be an obstacle to the various wheeled elements of the force, so some of the female tanks were equipped with powered winches, driven from the secondary gears on the right side. Having reached the top of the wall these tanks would position themselves facing inland and draw up the guns, transport and sledges laden with stores.

Whether Operation *Hush* would have worked or not is debatable, but it was a brave conception and highly innovative. In the end it was a wash-out due to the failure of the main offensive, but the winch tanks proved extremely useful later for recovery work.

With the Egyptian Expeditionary Force
The first tank operation in the Middle East, at the second battle of Gaza (see New Vanguard 100), resulted in the loss of three tanks, which were replaced in due course by three of the Mark IV type, two male and one female. The battle known as Third Gaza was scheduled to begin on 1 November 1917 and, despite their numbers, the tanks were destined to play a significant part.

The preparations for battle were made far better than on the previous occasion. There was time for adequate reconnaissance and pre-battle cooperation with the infantry, although the six tanks earmarked to lead the attack had far too many objectives to complete and the two held in reserve were overloaded with stores to deliver before they could clear the

Undoubtedly the best picture yet seen of one of the Operation Hush winching tanks still in use in 1918, presumably in a recovery role. The winch, driven off the starboard side secondary gears and tucked behind the extra panel of armour, is believed to have been supplied by John Fowler & Company of Leeds, who specialized in cable plough equipment.

decks for action. The battle actually began by moonlight, which normally spelled disaster for tanks, but here it was so bright that there were no problems. Even so, three tanks of the first wave became ditched and had to be abandoned, while the reserve tanks got into trouble because of stores piled on top catching fire due to their proximity to the exhaust. None of the tanks arrived in time to do any fighting; in the end it did not matter since the entire battle was well planned and well executed to the extent that within three days the defeated Turkish Army pulled out.

Once the battle was over the three abandoned tanks were recovered and restored, but they would not see action again. The nature of the terrain and the speed of the subsequent advance saw them excluded from future combat and in due course Maj Norman Nutt's detachment returned home.

The battle of Cambrai

Cambrai and the Mark IV tank are inseparable. Not that the tanks could have functioned without the aid of other arms, but they were the main focal point of the battle and it is worth remembering that Cambrai had to be structured around them, not the other way around. In other words, it was the limitations of the Mark IV tank – its speed, range and manoeuvrability – as much as its potential that dictated the pace of things. It is also worth recording that from October 1917 male tanks were issued with case shot, which proved to be an effective anti-infantry round. An official stowage list states that each male tank was to carry 184 shells and 20 rounds of case.

There is little purpose in covering Cambrai in detail here; it has been picked over in print innumerable times. Since we must concentrate on the tanks, then it would be best to notice what was special about them in this battle and how they were adapted for the occasion. However, first a small matter of figures. The tank battalions were shared, unequally, between three brigades. All nine battalions of the Tank Corps then in France took part and each battalion had, theoretically, 42 Mark IV tanks. Of these, in

most cases, 24 took part in the initial attack with 12 more to follow through to the second objective and six held in reserve. This gives us a total of 378 fighting tanks. In addition there were 54 supply tanks and nine wireless tanks divided between the three tank brigades, while among the fighting tanks already recorded 32 were equipped as wire cutters, two as light bridge carriers for the cavalry and one loaded with spare reels of telephone line since this material, liberally strewn all over the field, was often broken (usually by the tanks themselves) or 'borrowed' for unofficial purposes. All of these tanks had to be delivered to the area by rail, a process that involved nine trains each day for four days, each train carrying 12 tanks. The railhead was a vast marshalling yard known as 'Plateau', where as each train arrived it was unloaded so that tanks could be fitted with their fascines, then reloaded and despatched to advanced railheads nearer to the frontline.

Zero Hour was at 6.20am on 20 November 1917 and simultaneously with a brief but violent artillery barrage, the first wave of tanks moved off in the misty, pre-dawn darkness. Near the centre of the line a male tank with the improbable name of *Hilda* (Lt T. H. Leach commanding) carried the Tank Corps commander, BrigGen Hugh Elles, flying the red, brown and green Tank Corps colours from the top hatch. It is by such actions that *l'esprit de corps* is fostered. Cambrai was not a success in the long run but its initial impact was remarkable, so much so that Cambrai Day continues to be celebrated by the Royal Tank Regiment. And it is probably indicative that the greatest reverse, when a battery of 7.7cm guns trained in the anti-tank role knocked out 16 British tanks on the Flesquieres Ridge, has somehow become part of the British legend. It is also worth pointing out, to maintain a sense of balance, that the published histories of most British infantry divisions that took part in the battle hardly mention tanks at all.

Each one of these tanks had a 1.5-ton fascine perched on top of its cab and Cambrai was the only occasion when this device was used by tanks in this way. A quick glance at the statistics would probably help to explain why. In its normal form, as a modest bundle of sticks, the fascine is probably as old as warfare. Teams of sappers would carry them forward and throw them into ditches or trenches that might hold up the advance.

Mark IV tanks of D (on the left) and C battalions at Plateau railhead on the eve of Cambrai, with their fascines in place. It says a lot for the diligence of the Royal Flying Corps that this huge concentration of machines was never spotted from the air by the Germans, otherwise it would have given the whole game away.

Fins, near Gouzeaucourt on the
southern edge of the Cambrai
battlefield, was a railhead for the
start of the battle. Here it serves
the same function after the
battle as tanks are loaded up
and sheeted down for their
journey back to winter quarters.

Indeed they had been used in this way to fill the Steenbeek creek during
the attack on St Julien. By comparison the Cambrai fascines were
monsters, each one composed of 75 normal fascines bundled together
and then squeezed tight by loops of chain hauled by two tanks pulling in
opposite directions. All told some 400 tons (406 tonnes) of light timber
was extracted from the Forest of Crécy, which resulted in 22,000 small
fascines, sufficient for about 300 tanks. But it did not end there.

Techniques had to be devised for lifting the fascines onto the tanks
and then releasing them at the right time. Once again Central Workshops
had to turn to and manufacture the fittings, which included securing
chains, a quick-release mechanism and a lever inside the tank to operate
it. The drill was that as each tank approached its allotted section of the
extra-wide Hindenburg Line trenches, the driver would hold the tank on
the brake as it began to tip forward while the commander reached behind
him and jerked the special lever to release the fascine into the trench,

The crib, essentially a lighter,
reusable fascine, was rarely
seen on Mark IV tanks, but this
female with a broken track is
carrying one during the attack
on the Hindenburg Line on 27
September 1918 in support of
the Canadians.

whereupon the tank drove across it. Where they were used they appear to have worked perfectly well, but they were a one-shot commodity – they could not be recovered and used again.

In theory the wire-cutting tanks would be considered next in importance to the fascines. The British High Command had high hopes for Cambrai and visualized a total breakthrough of the German defence system through which they intended to send mounted cavalry. Unlike infantry, however, the cavalry could not negotiate wire entanglements, even flattened entanglements, at all. Thus on certain sections of the front tanks would pass through the wire in pairs, dragging huge grapnels that tore through the entanglements and, as the towing tanks peeled off right and left, ripped the wire clean out of the ground. It worked so well that not a trace of wire remained in the gaps, or so they say. In the event this was all to no purpose. For reasons that need not concern us here, the cavalry was unable to take advantage of the opportunity, so its contribution to the battle was limited.

Supply tanks had already proved their value. Those at Cambrai certainly included some of the earlier types along with others based upon redundant Gun Carrier machines, but the Mark IV versions were something of a special case. They had simple, unarmoured sponsons based on the shape of the original male type, but the interior was more scientifically arranged to carry more equipment and in a tidier fashion. Wire mesh screens were erected to keep the stores from falling upon the engine or the crew but the difficulty, as far as the latter were concerned, was that this prevented them from moving around inside the tank. Thus the gearsmen, having climbed in through the sponson doors, were more or less trapped near the secondary gears while the driver and commander could only clamber in or out through a new hatch fitted in the cab roof. In addition to the load they could carry inside and on top, the supply tanks were also equipped to tow trains of store sledges, similar to those designed for Operation *Hush*, and these became yet another burden on the overworked staff at Central Workshops, since it was not possible to have them made in Britain.

This Mark IV female, probably training with American infantry, demonstrates its ability to deal with barbed-wire entanglements, but note that in the front of the sponson the Lewis gun has been replaced by a rifle fitted with a grenade-launching cup.

Regarding the wireless tanks, it is not clear whether, at this stage of the war, they were of the Mark IV type or redundant veterans of 1916. None of the surviving photographs, mostly of knocked-out tanks, appear to show them, although it is known that the one and only cable-carrying tank was a Mark IV of G Battalion named *Galway*.

Cambrai failed in the long run due to a lack of adequate reserves on the part of the British and increasingly stubborn German resistance, including their use of mobile anti-aircraft guns in the anti-tank role. The German counter-attack at the end of the month enabled them to clear many broken down and abandoned tanks from the area, either for their own use or as a source for spare parts. Bearing in mind that only a few of the abandoned tanks were runners, the system arranged for their recovery was extremely ingenious, although it would only work on good ground and preferably near roads.

The Germans designed a system of rollers, each approximately the width of a tank and attached to a sub-frame. Each tank was raised on four heavy-duty jacks while two of these rollers were pushed underneath and the whole ensemble drawn to the railhead by a steam traction engine. The recovered tank was parked astride the railway, raised again while the rollers were towed away and a railway wagon shunted underneath instead.

One tank, in working condition, was taken to Berlin and demonstrated for the Kaiser, while the remainder were moved to a factory near Charleroi in occupied Belgium, where a repair facility was established. Precise figures are not available, but it appears that of some 50 tanks dragged off the Cambrai battlefield around 30 were restored to operational condition. The female tanks were first in service since, following difficulties with the 08 Pattern Maxim machine gun, the majority retained their Lewis guns, suitably modified to fire German ammunition. The male tanks presented a greater problem. The majority had already been stripped of their 57mm guns as they lay on the battlefield and it was some time before they could be rearmed with 57mm Nordenfelt guns taken from captured Belgian stocks. There is some photographic evidence to show that the 13mm anti-tank rifle, the so-called T-gewehr, could be fired from a female sponson and at least one tank had the front machine-gun mounting adapted to accept this weapon. For some reason the Germans elected to cram a crew

One of two tanks knocked out in Bourlon Wood, Cambrai, on 23 November 1917. This one has suffered a major internal explosion that has bulged out the floor and broken open the front end. Of technical interest, since it is not normally seen, is the way the spaced armour behind the petrol tank is attached at the bottom.

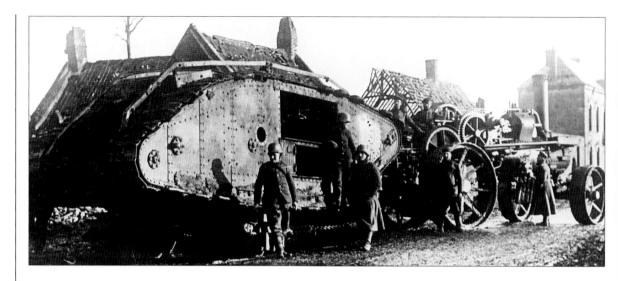

of 12 into their Mark IV tanks, although one photograph purports to show a tank modified to make it possible to operate the secondary gears from the front seats. There is no indication given of how it worked and, to judge from the photograph, the equipment looks too flimsy for the job and may have been nothing more than a mechanical indicator for the gearsmen. The Germans are also reported to have fitted a hatch in the cab roof of their captured tanks.

The Germans created a tank training area at St Amand, close by Charleroi, and raised up to six detachments to operate captured tanks alongside their own home-grown design, the A7V. As New Vanguard 127: *German Panzers 1917–18* explains in more detail, The Mark IV *Beutepanzers* not only outnumbered A7Vs in German service, they generally proved to be more reliable and better suited to the conditions. However, there were many delays in the restoration process, which seems to have had quite a low priority, and, although they saw some service, the German tanks appeared too late to achieve very much, were not always used in the most advantageous way and were never available in sufficient numbers.

This rather dark picture shows a stripped female machine being recovered by German troops in the aftermath of Cambrai using a large traction engine and two sets of rollers, linked by chain, to support the otherwise immobile tank. This tank is believed to be 158, which caught fire in Bourlon village on 24 November 1917 and had to be abandoned.

A very rare view of an A7V and captured Mark IV together, both in a semi-dismantled state, probably at Charleroi after its capture by the British at the end of the war. The A7V is believed to be 503; the Mark IV has not been identified.

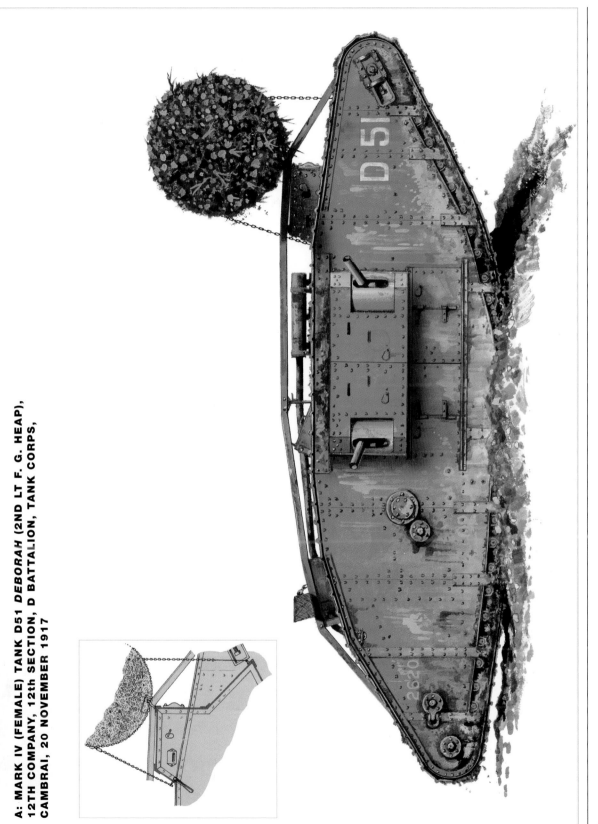

A: MARK IV (FEMALE) TANK D51 *DEBORAH* (2ND LT F. G. HEAP), 12TH COMPANY, 12th SECTION, D BATTALION, TANK CORPS, CAMBRAI, 20 NOVEMBER 1917

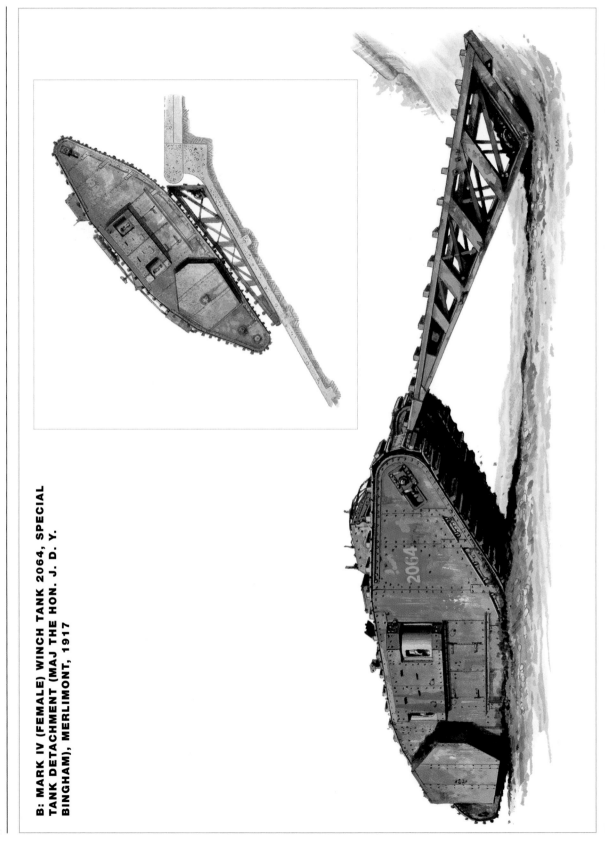

B: MARK IV (FEMALE) WINCH TANK 2064, SPECIAL TANK DETACHMENT (MAJ THE HON. J. D. Y. BINGHAM), MERLIMONT, 1917

B

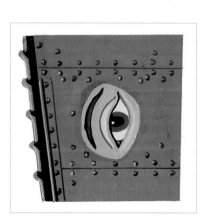

C1: MARK IV SUPPLY TANK *AULD REEKIE*, TANK CORPS CENTRAL WORKSHOPS, FRANCE, 1917

C2: MARK IV (MALE) TANK *FAN-TAN*, 6TH BATTALION, TANK CORPS

D: MARK IV TANK UNDER CONSTRUCTION, JOHN BROWN & COMPANY, CLYDEBANK, MAY 1917

SPECIFICATIONS

Crew: eight

Weight: 27.9 tons (28.4 tonnes)

Power to Weight ratio: 3.7bhp/ton (2.8kW/tonne)

Overall length: 26ft 3in. (8m)

Overall width (male): 13ft 6in. (4.11m)

Overall height: 7ft 11in. (2.43m)

Engine: Daimler/Knight sleeve valve, water-cooled straight six 105hp (78kW) @1,000rpm

Transmission: two-speed and reverse primary box with secondary two-speed selectors on the output shafts

Fuel capacity: 70 gallons (318 litres)

Max. speed: 3.69mph (5.95km/h)

Radius of action: 35 miles (56km)

Fuel consumption: 2.08 gallons per mile (5.9 litres/km)

Ground pressure: 12.6/74.8 kg/sq cm

Trench-crossing capability: 11ft 5in. (3.5m)

Armament: two 6-pdr (57mm) 23-calibre, quick-firing guns and four 7.62mm Lewis air-cooled machine guns

Muzzle velocity (6-pdr): 1,348ft/sec (411mps)

Max. range (6-pdr): 7,978 yards (7,300m)

Ammunition: solid shot, high explosive & case

Ammunition stowage (male): 332 6-pdr, 6,272 mg

KEY

1 Radiators
2 Differential lock lever
3 Differential housing
4 Primary gearbox
5 Oil tank
6 Engine governor
7 Coolant circulation system
8 Inlet manifold
9 Crank handle extension shaft
10 Starter drive chain
11 Starter engagement lever
12 Primary gear lever

13 Steering brake levers
14 Foot brake pedal
15 Foot clutch pedal
16 Hand assist lever for clutch pedal
17 Rear hull plate
18 Track plates
19 Drive sprockets
20 Final drive chain
21 Rear roof hatch coaming
22 Rear roof panels
23 Shaft used for hull alignment
24 Hole for track roller spindle

25 Rear camouflage support bracket
26 Cab side vision slit
27 Cab side loophole
28 Upper track support rail
29 Cab front vision slit
30 Forward camouflage support bracket
31 Commander's visor opening
32 Aperture for Lewis machine-gun
   mounting
33 Slot for idler spindle and track adjuster
34 Location of track switch plate
35 Track rollers

E1: MARK IV (MALE) TANK *LODESTAR*, 12TH BATTALION, TANK CORPS, FRANCE 1918

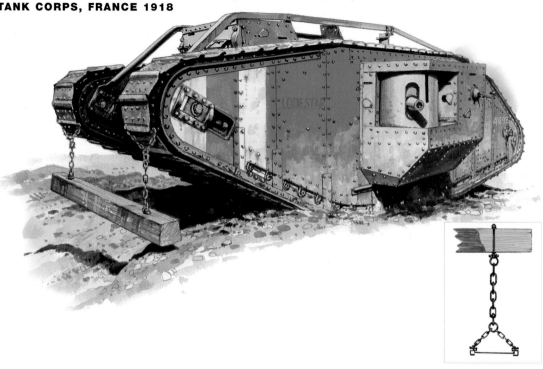

E2: MARK IV (FEMALE) *BEUTEPANZER DORA,* BAYERISCHER ARMEE-KRAFTWAGEN-PARK 20, CHARLEROI, BELGIUM, 1918

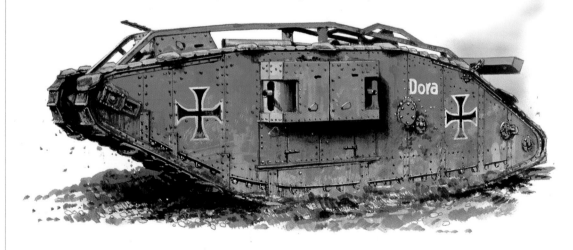

F1: MARK IV (MALE) TANK *EXCELLENT*, WHALE ISLAND, PORTSMOUTH, 1940

F2: MARK IV (MALE) TANK *EGBERT*, NATIONAL WAR SAVINGS COMMITTEE TOUR, ENGLAND, 1918

F

MECHANICAL IMPROVEMENTS

The feeling that the Mark I to Mark IV tanks were underpowered was quite common and, for the long term, a new, more powerful engine was being designed. In the meantime, the Royal Naval Air Service provided an aero engine expert to see what might be done with the Daimler. Lt W. O. Bentley, whose name would later become synonymous with large sports cars, had a particular interest in the use of aluminium pistons to improve performance and when these were applied to the Daimler, in conjunction with a new carburettor, they increased the compression ratio from 4.2:1 to 4.75:1 and raised the power from 105 to 125hp (78 to 93kW). This modification was applied to many of the later production tanks, but in practice it had a severe drawback. In careless hands the extra power stressed the secondary gear shafts, which buckled under the strain. The majority of 125hp (93kW) tanks, therefore, entered service as supply tanks, which did not suffer such hard usage.

Another significant change, introduced part way through production, concerned the radiator. To begin with tanks were fitted with the original Daimler envelope type, derived from the Foster-Daimler tractor and used in the earlier tanks. These were replaced in later machines by a pair of 'gilled tube' radiators which gave better air and water circulation and therefore better cooling. In either case the radiator was cooled by a belt-driven fan that drew in air from the body of the tank, thus alleviating the ghastly conditions to some extent. Having passed through the radiator air was ejected through a louvred panel at the back.

While the fascines used at Cambrai certainly worked they were a clumsy solution to the problem, being heavy, labour intensive and a one-shot trick since they could not be recovered and used again. One alternative to the problem of wider trenches was to stretch the tank, although this would raise problems connected with steering. Fosters came up with a device known as the 'Tadpole Tail', which extended the track frames rearwards but, most of the time at least, remained clear of the ground. The attachment lengthened the tank by 2.74m (9ft) and required 28 more track plates on each side and an extension of the chain

From the rear are visible the new-style radiators, the drive sprockets, plus the skid rails and flanged rollers that carried the top run of the tracks. The tank on the left is in a more advanced state of construction.

drive to the rear sprocket. As is often the case, the modified tank worked adequately on trials but did not stand up so well to continued use, the tail being too light and flexible to remain rigid enough. A substantial number of these tails were made and shipped to France, but there is no evidence to suggest that they were employed on service tanks. The original modified Mark IV, a male machine, was used for various trials, including sledge-towing and the mounting of a Newton mortar in the gap between the rear frames and set to fire forwards, over the tank. The Tadpole Tail was also fitted experimentally to the Mark V tank, but it does not appear to have been popular with Central Workshops personnel in France, who came up with a solution of their own. This is more normally associated with the Mark V, but there are some references that suggest that at an early stage in the process a Mark IV was adapted by having an extra 1.82m (6ft) section of hull inserted just to the rear of the gun sponson aperture, which effectively extended the body of the tank.

A number of Mark IV tanks had by 1917 joined the earlier models at Bovington Camp for use as training machines. Most were identical to the fighting tanks in France, although they normally lacked the undirecting beam and support rails and displayed a large, three-digit number probably in white on both sides and sometimes at the front and rear as well. Bovington also carried out various experiments on its own initiative, many of which dealt with methods of cutting barbed wire or finding other ways of carrying infantry, although there is no certainty that this particularly involved Mark IV machines. One trial that certainly did was a curious arrangement in which an undirecting beam, supported by the usual rails, was actually carried around the tank on two loops of heavy duty Renolds chain that seems to have been driven via a cross-shaft at the rear, linked to the final drive. It is not entirely clear how, or indeed whether, it worked. Given the stresses and strains involved the device does not look strong enough, but it would have reduced the risks associated with attaching an undirecting beam under fire and it appears to have survived to the end of the war.

A portable tank crane, in fact nothing more than a jib and chain hoist that could be fitted to the nose of any heavy tank, was commonly

The Mark IV male Tadpole Tail, posed at Dollis Hill to display its rear extensions and a 6-in. mortar mounted to fire over the tank. Tests were also carried out on firing mortars from inside male sponsons.

Photographed at Bovington, this rear view of a tank with chain-operated unditching beam equipment shows how the chains were powered by a special cross-shaft and extra sprockets at the rear. Note that a fascine is also fitted, but whether that was also activated by the chain gear is not clear.

seen on Mark IV tanks in the salvage role. They were particularly useful in workshops, but Bovington went one better and mounted a massive, gear-operated winch on the back of one Mark IV supply tank, which was evidently used on a regular basis around the workshops towards the end of the war.

In an increasingly technological war the concept of cooperation between aircraft and tanks was explored. (Cooperation between the Royal Flying Corps and the Royal Artillery was already well established.) Tanks carried an identification number painted on top of the cab for reporting purposes, but any direct communication with aircraft was hampered by the poor visibility from inside the tanks and the engine noise. The two forces devised a system of signalling from plane to tank using long, paddle-like arms protruding from the sides of an aircraft in various combinations to signify a limited range of messages. How anyone

Number 466 was the unusual combination of a training tank with supply sponsons. It was used at Bovington as a crane tank with a standard jib. The big winch at the back operates the hoist instead of the usual chain system.

was expected to see this from inside a tank, never mind which tank was being addressed or how it responded, is unclear. In fact Capt Bernard Rice of 8 Squadron, Royal Flying Corps (RFC), reckoned that tanks were almost impossible to spot from the air unless you followed the tracks they had made.

Clearly, radio communication between aircraft and tank would be most desirable, but here the technology was severely limited. The RFC already had a lightweight transmitting set, but there was nothing equivalent for the tanks and in any case it would be defeated in a tank by the volume of noise. To test the ground–air radio a Mark IV male training tank was used, in conjunction with a BE2c, at the Biggin Hill experimental establishment, but the results do not appear to have been very successful. Even so, aircraft played a significant part in support of tanks during the Cambrai battle. Four RFC squadrons were earmarked for the ground-attack role and proved to be particularly effective when engaging enemy artillery batteries that were themselves deployed for anti-tank work.

This is the Mark IV supply tank used for aircraft-to-tank wireless communication trials at Biggin Hill towards the end of the war. The panel suspended by string between the front horns is presumably something to do with the receiving process.

More power

Still in pursuit of improved performance over and above what W. O. Bentley had provided, Albert Stern tried to persuade Daimler to come up with something better. They turned the offer down pleading pressure of work so, early in January 1917, Stern approached a young engineer named Harry Ricardo to see what he could offer. The story of the Ricardo engine belongs more properly to the saga of the Mark V tank, but it is mentioned here for what might have been. Ricardo's brief included the requirement that his new engine should fit into the same location as the Daimler, although more height was permitted so it was entirely possible to install the Ricardo engine into the Mark IV, and this was certainly done. Lists of experimental machines issued by the Mechanical Warfare Department at the end of the war included some Mark IVs described as having Ricardo engines, although nothing is said about transmissions.

Presumably if the 125hp (93kW) Daimler was too powerful for the secondary gear shafts of the Mark IV, the 150hp (112kW) Ricardo was even worse, but the installations may only have been for trials purposes and test crews presumably handled them with more care. Ultimately, of course, the plan was to operate the Ricardo engine in conjunction with Wilson's epicyclic transmission. If the full conversion had been carried out on the Mark IV, as it must have been for test purposes, the resulting production machines would have been designated Mark IVA. In November 1918 a list was compiled of the number of surviving Mark IV tanks, most of which were being held as reserves in France, and the plan was to fit these with the Wilson transmission while retaining the Daimler engine. This was never done because there was no need, but it is not clear whether the original Daimler gearbox was to be replaced as well.

The obvious advantages of the Wilson transmission notwithstanding, other options for mechanical improvement were still being considered through 1917. Apart from heat problems, the Williams-Janney hydraulic steering system had shown promise at Oldbury and an Edinburgh firm, Brown Brothers, were charged with perfecting it. They first applied it to a Mark IV tank, which may well have been one of the 11 dedicated experimental machines listed earlier. As a result an improved type, known as the Mark VII, was developed to prototype stage.

1918 – THE FINAL BATTLES

In January 1918 the tank battalions were instructed to alter their desig-nations from letters to numbers, A Battalion becoming 1st, B 2nd and so on. The New Year also witnessed a gradual eclipse of the supremacy of the Mark IV with the appearance of improved tanks from British factories and a potent rival in the German ranks. The Mark IV had plenty of fight left in it – this it showed right to the end – but the nature of the war was changing to one of more fluid conditions that the plodding Mark IV, with its cumbersome driving system, simply could not match.

This development is probably exemplified by the events of March–May 1918, the period of the two great German counter-attacks. Largely relieved of their commitments in the east by the Russian Revolution, the German High Command poured thousands more men into the Western

Front, intent on forcing a decision before vast new American armies could arrive to checkmate them.

The Allies were well aware that such an attack was impending and, beyond strengthening the traditional defences there was the question of what to do with the tanks. It was impossible to predict just where the attacks might fall. Therefore, in addition to keeping the bulk of the armour well back in reserve, and ultimately employing the crews as infantry Lewis gun teams, a number of tanks were retained in locations close to the frontline to be employed as what BrigGen Hugh Elles described as 'Savage Rabbits'. The idea was that as the German attack surged forwards these tanks would throw off their camouflage and dash out to attack them. In this role the tanks had some successes, but there were too many handicaps. For a start, Mark IV tanks were simply not designed to dash anywhere, but in addition German tactics involved the attackers swerving away from any serious resistance and looking for a weaker spot somewhere else. Many tanks were lost when they became cut off behind the advancing German line.

Towards the end of April the Germans had accumulated sufficient tanks of their own, both the A7V and some captured Mark IVs, to mount an attack on the Somme front. One of three A7V tanks, emerging from the town of Villers-Bretonneux, encountered three Mark IVs of 1st (A) Battalion which were patrolling the British line near the village of Cachy. Two of the British tanks, both females, were engaged by the German tank and forced to withdraw with serious damage. Meanwhile, the British male was manoeuvring for a good position and prepared to take on the A7V. One unfortunate feature of all British tanks of World War I was the total lack of any sprung suspension. This deficiency not only gave the crew a very harsh ride, it also transmitted vibrations to every part of the tank including the sighting telescope, which was rendered useless. The commander of tank A1, 2nd Lt Frank Mitchell, had the sense to halt and

This view of a Mark IV supply tank was taken in Hourges on the second day of the battle of Amiens, 9 August 1918. It appears to be waiting to go forward, well laden with stores. Meanwhile, German prisoners are bringing in a stretcher case.

his gunner managed to put a number of rounds through the German A7V No. 561 *Nixe* (Lt Wilhelm Biltz) of Assault Tank Detachment 2. Historically, this first tank-versus-tank fight is a significant although pyrrhic victory. Biltz abandoned his tank but later managed to retrieve it and withdraw some distance before it seized up. Frank Mitchell stayed in command of the field but his tank was soon hit by German artillery, disabled and abandoned.

By the summer of 1918 the majority of battalions had re-equipped with the new Mark V tank or were training to do so. Thus when the great battle of Amiens opened on 8 August the only Mark IVs to be seen would have been supply tanks. There were, however, two Tank Corps battalions, the 7th and 12th, which retained their Mark IVs and used them in some of the later battles. Fortunately the tanks were applied with a good deal of common sense. For example, at Bapaume on 21 August each type of tank was used to its best advantage. Thus the two Mark IV battalions led the way through the thinly held German outpost line and on to the second objective, where the more powerful Mark V and Mark V* machines took over. The Germans had taken up the idea of thinning out their frontline and keeping their main strength farther back in the hope that the attackers, by the time they reached the deeper lines, would have run out of steam. At Bapaume their main line of resistance was the embanked railway line that linked Albert with Arras. This was heavily defended but the new tanks were relatively fresh, despite running the gauntlet of a heavy German barrage, and broke through to create an opportunity for the lighter, faster Whippet tanks to undertake the third stage.

At Moeuvres on 27 September, 16 Mark IVs from 7th Battalion operated with the Canadian Corps in an attack that involved crossing the dry bed of the unfinished Canal du Nord which, in places, had a bank some 2.74m (9ft) high. All but one of the tanks, some of which had fought over the same ground at Cambrai nearly a year earlier, managed to climb

This unusual photograph shows a Mark IV female *Beutepanzer* that may have been a victim of the fighting on 8 October 1918. The legend on the side claims that it was captured by 12th Battalion and the damage to the side and front, not to mention the broken track, suggests that it has been in a fight. If so it would be one of the German 15th Battalion tanks that participated in the second tank-versus-tank action of the war.

the bank and roll into action. Even so, as a foretaste of future problems one of the tanks was disabled by a German mine buried in a roadway.

The last battle involving Mark IV tanks seems to have been towards the end of Second Cambrai on 8 October, when 12th Battalion had the unusual experience of confronting four Mark IV tanks in German hands near Niergnies. Accounts of the action are confusing and contradictory, but it may be that male tank L16 put one of the *Beutepanzers* out of action. The German tanks, or their supporting artillery, exacted some revenge and knocked out at least three of the British Mark IVs, including L16, while the crew of L8 used a captured German gun to smash another of the German tanks. When another Mark IV, albeit a female, rolled up from the British side, the remaining German tanks departed.

That was it as far as the fighting Mark IV tanks were concerned, but others may have remained in service as supply tanks. The last tank action of the war took place on 4 November 1918 in the area around the Mormal Forest. It was here that three supply tanks, which could easily have been Mark IVs, on a mission to deliver bridge-building material to the village of Landrecies, saw action. Approaching the site they discovered German troops still in occupation but decided to attack anyway, relying upon their appearance, and a single machine gun each. At the cost of one tank disabled, they captured a number of troops and chased the rest away. A week later the fighting came to an end.

POST-WAR

Almost coinciding with the battle of Cambrai, a pair of Mark IV tanks took part in the Lord Mayor's Show in the City of London in November 1917. Their popularity was so marked that a tank was also incorporated into an exhibition of weapons displayed in Trafalgar Square around the same time. To capitalize on the tanks' popularity, the National War Savings Committee organized a programme of travelling tanks that toured England and Wales selling War Bonds, and subsequently Victory Bonds, when the fighting was over. A similar scheme operated in Scotland. Impressive sums were raised and, to judge from the timetable, a lot of hard work was involved. Tanks travelled by rail and at every

Clearing the battlefield at the end of the war, a Mark IV supply tank assists in righting a badly damaged machine that looks as if it suffered a major internal explosion. Notice what appears to be a very large hatch on the cab roof of the wreck.

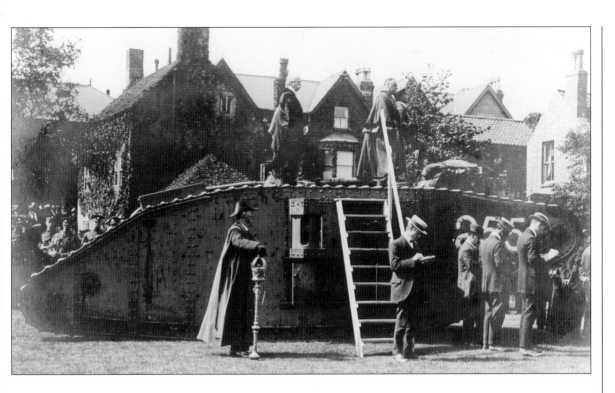

Mansfield in Nottinghamshire receives its 'War Bond' tank – female training machine 255 – on 21 May 1919 and the town council is out in force, as are the gentlemen of the press. The officer standing next to the mayor seems to be speaking, while the rest of the crew are lined up in front.

location the skeleton crew had to reinstate the sponsons (all five touring tanks were male machines), drive into town and spend a few hours acting as a platform for speakers and as a sales point for the Bonds. There appear to have been times when an individual tank managed two adjacent towns in a single day which must also have increased the burden for the overworked railways.

In 1919, with the agreement of the Tank Corps, the National War Savings Committee decided to offer redundant tanks to any community that had raised more than a certain sum per head of population. Some 265 communities in England and Wales were nominated, along with an uncertain number in Scotland. The majority accepted and delivery was arranged from Bovington. Female tanks were preferred since, without machine guns, they had no offensive potential for unruly elements in society bent on revolution. In each case the tank was delivered by rail from Bovington with a scratch crew and driven to its final resting place. Here the young officer gave an account of the particular tank's war record – almost always fictitious – disabled it mechanically and set off for home.

Some locations, mostly cities such as Coventry or Lincoln that were associated with the production of tanks, received male machines, but others were distributed to locations for more obvious reasons. For example, the Royal Naval Gunnery School HMS *Excellent* on Whale Island, Portsmouth, received a male tank in recognition of its help training tank gunners in the early days, and various communities in France were also recipients. Cambrai is a good example: having enjoyed close associations with the Tank Corps during the war, it also received Mark IVs. There were more than enough to spare.

The Mark IV was obsolete even before the war ended; it would have no place in the post-war army. For one thing, a considerable cloud hung over the future of the tank as a weapon, but in any case

immediate requirements, limited as they were, could easily be met by the vastly superior Mark V machines.

One Mark IV is known to have served in Ireland, while a dozen were supplied to the United States, although it is not clear what the Americans wanted them for. Others were donated as examples to certain Commonwealth countries and overseas Dominions such as Australia and Canada. Another was supplied to Japan, but whether as a gesture of Allied gratitude or a sample for future development it is not clear. One even ended up as a seaside attraction at Southend-on-Sea. Operated by a consortium of retired Tank Corps officers, and stripped of its sponsons, it had seats inside for those who wished to be deafened and a wooden upper deck for passengers who preferred fresh sea air. It appears to have done at least one season running up and down the beach, but it would have been a maintenance nightmare and it is doubtful if it ever returned a worthwhile profit to its proprietors.

Although it was in its infancy in 1918, the anti-tank mine was beginning to prove a serious threat and various German types were described in the *Tank Corps' Weekly Tank Notes*, the majority of which were based on buried artillery shells detonated by pressure. As a counter-measure, the obvious method of setting them off ahead of an approaching tank was some sort of

The Mark IV female presented to Barnsley, and displayed in Locke Park, is a genuine veteran; the unditching beam rails and red and white stripes are a giveaway. Though no proof has been found as yet, some evidence suggests that captured enemy artillery was donated to towns with Victoria Cross recipients, so the German 77mm gun in front of the tank might indicate this.

This is the only known photo of the Mark IV anti-mine roller, which is believed to have been completed at Christchurch at the end of the war. The rolls are clearly taken from a couple of steamrollers and are pivoted like castors. Why the tank is painted as it is, in contrast to the sponson, is not clear.

heavy roller device and a Mark IV female was used for one such experiment at Christchurch. Two hefty wooden beams extended forwards from the track horns. At the end of each was a complete front roller drum from a commercial steam road roller. It must have been very hard work for the tank, but the vehicle was completed too late to make any difference.

The vast majority of war surplus tanks were simply shipped back to Bovington and scrapped, although a significant number still remained on the Western Front, too damaged to move but too much of a nuisance to leave behind. Thus the Tank Corps raised a special salvage detachment which, for many months after the end of hostilities, worked steadily across the battlefields, blowing up wrecks where it was safe to do so or, in a few cases, burying them where it was not.

Most of the captured tanks used by the Germans were recaptured, although two female Mark IVs were operated by Freikorps forces in Berlin in 1919 in an attempt to overawe dissidents. These were then handed over to the Allied Control Commission, although another female machine, sent to Daimler at Stuttgart as a pattern for German designs, appeared briefly in 1920 before it, too, was repossessed.

That might have been it as far as the Mark IV was concerned had it not been for the threatened German invasion of 1940. Serving at Whale Island at this time SubLt Menhinnick, RN, looked over an old male tank and wondered if it might not be put back into working order for local defence. Missing parts were taken from another Mark IV then located on Southsea Common and the old machine was soon running again. A special cupola with a machine gun for anti-aircraft use was added on top of the hull and the tank repainted in contemporary military colours. On one occasion it ventured across to the mainland, using the causeway that is exposed at low tide, and here, according to legend, it collided with a private car and further use was banned. Perhaps it is fitting that it should be the Royal Navy that last used a World War I tank. After all, they had been responsible for its introduction.

A number of towns and cities in France with strong Tank Corps associations also received tanks. Cambrai was an obvious choice, and to mark the importance of the occasion the city's legendary figures *Martin et Martine* have come down from their places on the Hotel de Ville to greet the tank.

COLOUR PLATE COMMENTARY

CAMOUFLAGE

In a landscape that was composed almost entirely of churned-up soil, there was little scope for any of the more exotic forms of camouflage on the Mark IV. The tanks had been painted a medium brown since early 1917 and although some patterned schemes have been identified from photographs, they are rare and show no signs of standardization. In any case, by the time various identification numbers had been painted on and crews had adorned their tanks with individual decorations or unit symbols, camouflage was a bit of a waste of time. Indeed there is a case for suggesting that in action it was better for tanks to be seen. Lying up prior to a battle was another matter and each tank was provided with a large camouflage net, suited to the area in which they were to hide. In October 1917, for example, 4th Battalion records that it was issued with nets that represented brick rubble, rather than trees or vegetation, in order to lie up in ruined villages. Special brackets on top of the cab and at the rear were standard fittings on the Mark IV to support these nets.

Protecting the tanks from aerial observation was another problem. The tanks could be adequately camouflaged at rest using the nets, although the Germans made careful study of the shadows that a tank would cast. On the move it was more difficult since the tracks, as they passed around the top of the hull, caught the light on a sunny day where they were worn silver and almost flashed up signals to the aircraft. One attempt to counter this by fitting an extensive frame and net arrangement over the top must have been more trouble than it was ever worth. In any case there was also a requirement for tanks to be seen and reported by friendly aircraft, so most of them had large unit numbers painted in white on top of the cab for that purpose.

A difficult picture to explain; a Mark IV male with red and white stripes and an odd pattern of markings on the sponson. A large baulk of timber, which may be an unditching beam, is stowed lengthwise on top and a soldier in a curious mixture of uniforms is leaning against it. At the front a name and number appear to have been painted out.

A: MARK IV (FEMALE) TANK D51 *DEBORAH* (2ND LT F. G. HEAP), 12TH COMPANY, 12TH SECTION, D BATTALION, TANK CORPS, CAMBRAI, 20 NOVEMBER 1917

Deborah is shown in the typical khaki brown finish. The number D51 would be repeated on the rear of the fuel tank and on top of the cab roof. The name would be painted across the front.

The bulky fascine is in the launching position above the cab and this area has been partly sectioned to show how this was done. The fascine itself is tightly bound with chains and chains are also used to secure it to the towing bracket on the nose. It is held at the rear by a quick-release arrangement, activated by a red lever situated at the back of the cab. The fascine would be released just as the tank began to tilt forward into the trench. Until the fascine is dropped the tank is unable to make use of its unditching equipment.

Deborah was knocked out by German artillery in Flesqueries and buried during battlefield clearance at the end of the war. It was rediscovered and recovered by local historian Philippe Gorczynski in 1997 and is now on display in the village.

B: MARK IV (FEMALE) WINCH TANK 2064, SPECIAL TANK DETACHMENT (MAJ THE HON. J. D. Y. BINGHAM), MERLIMONT, 1917

Operation *Hush* was a proposed amphibious landing on the Flanders coast in conjunction with the advance of General Rawlinson's Fourth Army during Third Ypres (July–November 1917). It was an example of amazing ingenuity devised to overcome a series of difficulties. Once the nine tanks were ashore, three tanks from each of three landing pontoons would be faced with a sloping sea wall, capped with an outward curving lip. The slope of the wall was not steep, but it was known to be coated with slimy seaweed.

To deal with this obstacle each tank was fitted with special, claw-like track attachments that dug into the concrete and prevented slipping. Projecting from the front of each tank was a wedge-shaped ramp on wheels, which the tank pushed ahead of itself until the ramp became wedged beneath the lip.

German crews train on captured Mark IV tanks at St Amand in Belgium. The Germans made far more use of interesting camouflage patterns than did the Tank Corps but then, for practical purposes, were obliged to adorn their tanks with large black crosses.

Here the ramp was released and remained jammed under the lip while the tank proceeded to climb over it in a series of jerks until it pitched over the top. Those tanks fitted with winches were now used to haul other vehicles and equipment over the wall.

The training wall was built at Merlimont, but in the end the operation never took place.

C1: MARK IV SUPPLY TANK *AULD REEKIE*, TANK CORPS CENTRAL WORKSHOPS, FRANCE, 1917

Supply tanks were workhorses with no glamour and few exciting stories to tell, yet without them tank operations would have been a lot more difficult. Most were official conversions from the 125hp (93kW) versions of the Mark IV that had been devised by Lt W. O. Bentley. Although the improved performance was welcome it could damage the gears if used violently in fighting tanks. It was thus more suited to the steady driving of supply tanks, despite the fact that they were often well laden and even towing supply sledges.

This typical example is finished in the inevitable khaki brown, relieved by the name at the front and the word SUPPLY, in bold white letters on the sides of the special sponsons. Photographs show some tanks with the word BAGGAGE here instead, but there is no obvious explanation. It is not possible to tell if this practice applies only to certain battalions or if it was meant to be slightly less revealing to the enemy than SUPPLY.

Supply tanks were also known as tank tenders and each one was capable of carrying 5 tons of stores, sufficient to re-supply five fighting tanks that might otherwise be forced to pull out of battle.

C2: MARK IV (MALE) TANK *FAN-TAN*, 6TH BATTALION, TANK CORPS

The donation of a tank with funds raised in Malaya subsequently attracted a good deal of mythology, although in fact it seems to have been managed almost entirely in Britain. The tank is shown here as it was when posing for a set of publicity photographs. There is a brass plate on the front with details of the donation, a fierce and colourful dragon beneath it and an eye painted on each side near the front. This reflected the oriental practice of painting eyes on boats so that they could 'see' where they were going.

At this display the tank was also fitted with three unusual air-cooled machine guns, apparently designed by Vickers, although they were never adopted for tanks. Tank No.2341 was built by Fosters of Lincoln and was issued to F (later 6th) Battalion. It served as *Fly-Paper* under 2nd Lt J. M. Oke, but was renamed *Fan-Tan* by the time of Cambrai, where it was commanded by Lt H. A. Aldridge. It remained with the battalion until June 1918 when the unit converted to Whippets.

It was hoped to present the tank to Malaya after the war, but there is no evidence that this ever happened.

D: MARK IV TANK UNDER CONSTRUCTION, JOHN BROWN & COMPANY, CLYDEBANK, MAY 1917

This illustration is derived from a photograph of a Mark IV tank being assembled. At this stage all the hull plates are in natural metal and long steel rods are being used to line up frames to ensure accuracy. The top plate is yet to be fitted, but this cannot be done before the engine assembly has been dropped into place.

The engine, gearbox and differential have been delivered from Daimler in Coventry. They are assembled together on a sub-frame complete with all driving controls and the radiator. Once these elements are installed, the sides of the engine will be covered in with sheet-metal panels and an exhaust stack will be fitted linking the manifold with a silencer on top.

Other items can be seen stacked around the tank. The rollers will be located in the series of holes along the bottom of

The female training tank fitted with a special tower to handle airships at the Royal Naval Air Station at Pulham in Norfolk. As the war ended the station petitioned the Tank Board for a Mark V machine, which was no doubt regarded as easier to handle for this difficult task, but this request was turned down.

the frames, along with track-adjusting idlers at the front and track drive sprockets at the rear. Finally the tracks will be fitted, the tank lowered to the ground and driven out of the building. In Glasgow new tanks were moved through the streets at night on large trailers, hauled by steam road locomotives to a specially prepared testing ground at Scotstoun.

For a cutaway view of an earlier tank, see Plate D, New Vanguard 100: *Mark I*.

E1: MARK IV (MALE) TANK *LODESTAR*, 12TH BATTALION, TANK CORPS, FRANCE 1918

Only two Tank Corps battalions, the 7th and 12th, retained Mark IV tanks right through until the end of the war. Both battalions supplied tanks for a rare night-time attack on the village of Gomiecourt on 23 August 1918 and later in operations over the old ground at Cambrai during the attack on the Hindenburg Line.

By this time all British tanks (including those operated by the 301st US Battalion) bore the white/red/white recognition stripes. These were normally painted on the front horns as shown, often on top of the cab and sometimes at the back as well. The Germans had salvaged so many British tanks from the original Cambrai battlefield that it was agreed to mark 'friendly' ones in this way. *Lodestar* survives in the Musée Royale de l'Armee in Brussels.

The unditching beam was invented in France and, in the case of Mark IV tanks, also fitted there by Tank Corps Central Workshops. It was carried on special rails running along the top of the hull and normally stowed near the back where it was easier to reach with some degree of protection for the crew. It was attached to each track by a form of stirrup that slid underneath but had to be bolted in place, a risky business under fire.

E2: MARK IV (FEMALE) *BEUTEPANZER DORA*, BAYERISCHER ARMEE-KRAFTWAGEN-PARK 20, CHARLEROI, BELGIUM, 1918

Dora (original identity unknown) seems to have been used for training and demonstration purposes before being issued to

a combat battalion. It appears to have retained the original British khaki brown colour, although all British markings have been painted out and replaced by iron crosses and a new name. The only other modification carried out by the Germans looks to be a hinged flap or hatch in the cab roof.

Most captured tanks were later finished in more exotic colour schemes; all were named and usually carried a circle device, in a colour appropriate to the battalion, on each side, but the style of national marking seems to have varied considerably. The provision of suitable machine guns for female tanks turned out to be a problem until a means was found to modify the original Lewis guns to chamber and fire German ammunition.

Dora's fate is not clear. The name does not appear in any subsequent battalion records so it may well be that the tank was renamed at some point. One trustworthy source suggests that *Dora* carried the number 101 and served with Battalion 11 and may later have been rechristened *Lotte* and issued to Battalion 14.

The T-gewehr anti-tank rifle was primarily an infantry weapon but some were carried in tanks. It fired a 13mm round and had a fierce recoil, but the effective range was little more than 91.4m (100 yards).

F1: MARK IV (MALE) TANK *EXCELLENT*, WHALE ISLAND, PORTSMOUTH, 1940

In addition to those tanks donated to municipalities around Britain as a reward for fund raising, some were supplied to establishments that had assisted with the development of tanks and the Tank Corps. HMS *Excellent*, the Royal Naval Gunnery School in Portsmouth Harbour, naturally received a

A nicely constructed photo of Tank 119 *Julian* on one of its sales tours. The young lady in the sponson will stamp the customers' cards while payment will be completed at a nearby bank or post office. We are also treated to a useful view of the interior of a male sponson door.

male tank for assisting with the training of tank gunners and the evidence suggests that it was a training tank from Bovington.

During the invasion scare period in the summer of 1940, a young officer from Whale Island restored the tank to running order, fitted it with a special Lewis gun mounting on top and prepared it for further action. It was finished in the two-tone green colour scheme favoured for tanks at this time, christened *Excellent* and to make a point had the letters 'R.N.' in white across the front and a large White Ensign flying at the back. Legend has it that it made one 'run ashore', damaged a private car and was quickly withdrawn.

This tank, fully restored to its original condition, is now a prized exhibit at the Tank Museum and a star of the BBC TV series *Soldiers* of 1983.

F2: MARK IV (MALE) TANK *EGBERT*, NATIONAL WAR SAVINGS COMMITTEE TOUR, ENGLAND, 1918

Quite how or where *Egbert* came by its damage is not clear. An *Egbert II* was with 5th Battalion at Cambrai, but it is not possible to say whether this was the same tank or not. Whatever the cause, *Egbert* shows signs of being hit at least twice by artillery fire, but, such is the lottery of these things, not being put out of action. At some point, probably in 1918, *Egbert* was returned to Britain and joined the team of 'Travelling Tanks' touring the country on behalf of the National War Savings Committee.

All of the other tanks in this group were immaculate training machines from Bovington, so *Egbert* seems to have been a considerable hit with the public; it had seen active service and even had the scars to prove it. The tanks toured by rail from town to town, were driven to suitable locations and then used as platforms for speakers and as booths for the pledging of War Bonds.

After the war it was agreed that *Egbert* should be awarded to the town that had contributed most, on a per head of population basis, which turned out to be Hartlepool in County Durham, where it remained on display for many years.

G: MARK IV (FEMALE) TANK *BRITANNIA*, NEW YORK CITY, 25 OCTOBER 1917

Tanks were despatched to a number of countries for publicity purposes, among which Australia, Canada and the United States have been identified. The American tank *Britannia* was shipped over in the summer of 1917 and in production terms must have been an early machine. It went with a specially selected British crew and took part in a number of events. On 25 October 1917 it formed part of a parade through New York City, escorted by armoured cars of the New York National Guard. This painting is based upon a spectacular photograph of *Britannia* rolling down Fifth Avenue, flying the Union Jack and the Stars and Stripes, with the distinctive shape of the famous 'Flat Iron' building in the background.

Heroland was a very American affair, a spectacular piece of showmanship intended to entertain the public, while educating them with regard to the war.

Tank 130 *Nelson* guarded by a sentry and a police constable along with two of its crew on a War Bond sales tour. It is shown here with a number of other weapons. Unfortunately the location has not yet been identified.

INDEX